THIS BOOK
BELONGS TO:

_____

GROWTH MINDSET JOURNAL FOR TEENS

Embrace Challenges, Build Resilience, Self-Reflect, and GROW

Christopher Taylor, MA, LMFT

ROCKRIDGE
PRESS

First Rockridge Press trade paperback edition 2022

Rockridge Press and the Rockridge Press logo are trademarks or registered trademarks of Callisto Media Inc. and/or its affiliates in the United States and other countries and may not be used without written permission.

For general information on our other products and services, please contact our Customer Care Department within the United States at (866) 744-2665, or outside the United States at (510) 253-0500.

Paperback ISBN: 978-1-68539-242-0

Manufactured in the United States of America

Interior and Cover Designer: Lisa Realmuto
Art Producer: Maya Melenchuk
Editor: Jeanann Pannasch
Production Editor: Cassie Gitkin
Production Manager: Lanore Coloprisco

All illustrations used under license from Shutterstock and iStock.

10 9 8 7 6 5 4 3 2 1 0

CONTENTS

WELCOME TO YOUR JOURNAL

Hi! Let me welcome you to your growth mindset journal. Whoever you are and whatever you're going through, you can enjoy and benefit from this journal. It was written for *you*. I hope you're excited! You are about to embark on an incredible journey.

My name is Chris Taylor. I am a mental health therapist who has been working with teens for the past 20 years. I have helped thousands of teens just like you believe in themselves and focus on what's possible. The key to realizing your biggest dreams is having a growth mindset, and in the pages ahead you will learn how to develop just that. You'll learn the skills necessary to build resiliency, reduce your stress, and pursue your passions with hope and optimism.

What Is a Growth Mindset?

There are two types of mindsets: growth and fixed. When we have a growth mindset, we believe we have the ability to learn, grow, and improve. We see obstacles as temporary and recognize that they offer us opportunities to learn how to overcome them. When we have a fixed mindset, we believe our abilities and talents are fixed, and therefore we cannot improve. We may fear challenges, feel our abilities are limited, and sense success is for others, not us.

Think of Thomas Edison. Obviously, we know him as the inventor of the lightbulb, but did you know that he holds the record for having the most patents? The funny thing is, almost all those patents are for lightbulb designs that failed! You see, Thomas Edison had a growth mindset. He saw even his failures as learning opportunities . . . and kept trying.

Everyone can learn to have a growth mindset—and it's easy if you know what to do. The core tenets, or beliefs, of a growth mindset are:

1. Effort and hard work are the keys to success, not just talent.

2. Mistakes and failures help you learn.

3. Unhelpful thoughts limit you.

4. You can create positive thoughts.

5. Frustration is a normal part of growth.

6. Comparison can hold you back.

7. Feedback and criticism are important for change.

8. Change is good.

Right now, you may have a growth mindset that crops up at times but is not always there. That's okay. This book will help you develop the skills to fully embrace a growth mindset. Journaling is an incredibly effective tool for exploring our fears and frustrations, and for uncovering our strengths.

I applaud you for taking this step. In the pages ahead, I challenge you to be truly honest with yourself. Know that once you are done with this journal, lasting change will be possible. I can't wait for you to get started, so let's jump in!

HOW TO USE THIS JOURNAL

This journal is for you to use however you like. You can work on the prompts in order or skip to the sections that spark your interest. Feel free to jump to an exercise that will bring your growth mindset alive. There is no right or wrong way to use this journal— no rules!

I know that life can get busy and stressful, so the goal is to make this journaling process fun. Find a cozy corner and play your favorite song. If you like, share what you learn with family and friends. Most of all, gift yourself the luxury of time to work on this journal. You deserve it.

Time to jump in and explore. No matter where you are in life right now, you'll find growth waiting. I'm so excited for you . . . let's go!

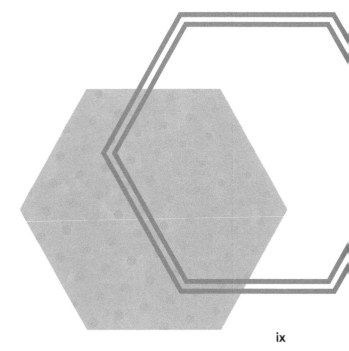

PART ONE
THE INCREDIBLE CHANGING BRAIN

Your brain is the world's most complex and amazing organ. It has one hundred billion neurons and more than one hundred trillion connections, all working to help you live your best life. In this section, we'll be exploring your habits, strengths, and values. We'll start creating the foundation for a solid growth mindset.

Let's explore the differences between a growth mindset and a fixed mindset. Below, circle either "Yes" or "No" based on how you feel about each statement.

1. Feedback makes me feel criticized and attacked. **Y** or **N**

2. I don't like to take risks and try new things. **Y** or **N**

3. It is impossible to learn new skills. **Y** or **N**

4. Success is predetermined in life. **Y** or **N**

5. I get frustrated when other people have success. **Y** or **N**

6. No matter how hard I work at something, I can't improve. **Y** or **N**

7. When something is hard to do, it's best to give up. **Y** or **N**

8. People are either intelligent or not, and that doesn't change. **Y** or **N**

9. People fail because they just don't have the talent. **Y** or **N**

10. It is important to me to always look smart, even if I don't know something. **Y** or **N**

All of these statements represent a fixed mindset. If you have a bunch of check marks in the "Yes" column, don't sweat it. Over the course of this journal, you'll be working to turn the yeses to nos! Bookmark this page, and come back periodically to see how you are doing.

The brain is ever-changing and always growing. Share an experience where you thought you knew pretty much everything about something (or someplace) but were surprised to find out there was so much more to learn.

_____

_____

_____

_____

_____

_____

_____

_____

_____

_____

_____

_____

Think of a time you overcame a challenge to reach a goal. What made you want to keep going? Did the hard part make the success better, worse, or the same?

_____

_____

_____

_____

_____

_____

_____

_____

_____

_____

_____

_____

_____

We change so much over the course of a lifetime. What recent changes have you made in responding to challenging situations? Maybe it's how you communicate with your parents or deal with disappointment. Do the changes fit within a growth mindset or a fixed mindset?

_____

_____

_____

_____

_____

_____

_____

_____

_____

_____

_____

_____

All you can do is focus on your own growth and joy and know that going at your own pace is the perfect pace.

—ZENDAYA COLEMAN

Think of a time when fear of being judged stopped you from doing something you used to love to do. How did having this fixed-mindset approach affect you emotionally? Would you go back and do it differently if you could?

_____

_____

_____

_____

_____

_____

_____

_____

_____

_____

_____

_____

_____

Have you ever been faced with a task so seemingly monumental that you walked away and didn't even try? Maybe it was a placement exam, or tryouts for a team or chorus. What was it that made you think you couldn't do it? Looking back, do you wish you had given it a shot? Is there a chance you still can?

_____

_____

_____

_____

_____

_____

_____

_____

_____

_____

_____

_____

Look over your responses to the last two prompts. Then turn to page viii and look at the core tenets of a growth mindset. Below, write down one or two approaches that could be applied to each situation if you were to face it again in the future.

_____

_____

_____

_____

_____

_____

_____

_____

_____

_____

_____

_____

Thoughts influence our emotions. Describe a time when you had a specific thought about your abilities that encouraged you to try harder and give more effort. What was that thought? Have you controlled your thoughts the same way since? Why or why not?

_____

_____

_____

_____

_____

_____

_____

_____

_____

_____

_____

_____

GROWTH MINDSET IN ACTION

Eliminate Excuses

Write down a couple of things you have always wanted to do but haven't yet done. Pick things you could realistically act on within a couple days. (For example, learning to play the guitar, not, say, traveling the world.) Once you have your things identified, write down all the negative thoughts that may get in the way of your doing them, such as "I won't be any good," "It's a stupid idea," or "People will laugh." Under each of those negative thoughts, write about a time that specific negative thought didn't end up being true. For example, if you wrote, "I won't be any good at making a birthday cake for my friend," write about a time you did something similar well, such as "I once baked great cupcakes for my aunt!" Do this for all the negative thoughts you've written. Now reread your success stories. It doesn't seem like you have many excuses anymore, does it? Bonus exercise: Take action and try one of your things this week.

What success are you most proud of in life, and why? Was it easy to achieve? What type of effort did you put in to achieve the success?

_____

_____

_____

_____

_____

_____

_____

_____

_____

_____

_____

_____

_____

Identify five areas of growth for the next year, such as being more organized, making a new friend, showing more kindness, improving your grades, or learning a new skill. Write out what you can commit to doing *now* that will help you achieve each goal.

1. _____

_____

2. _____

_____

3. _____

_____

4. _____

_____

5. _____

_____

Take this true/false quiz to test your understanding of the characteristics of a growth mindset.

1. A growth mindset is believing success comes from talent.   **T** or **F**

2. A growth mindset says that feedback is helpful for growth.   **T** or **F**

3. A growth mindset is believing you can grow intelligence.   **T** or **F**

4. A growth mindset says failure means you just can't do it.   **T** or **F**

5. A growth mindset means you keep trying even when you're frustrated.   **T** or **F**

6. A growth mindset says you should give up if it's too hard.   **T** or **F**

7. A growth mindset says you should try new things.   **T** or **F**

8. A growth mindset says taking risks is a bad idea.   **T** or **F**

9. A growth mindset is believing that failure is due to limited abilities.   **T** or **F**

10. A growth mindset means being threatened by the success of others.   **T** or **F**

1. F 2. T 3. T 4. F 5. T 6. F 7. T 8. F 9. F 10. F

GROWTH MINDSET IN ACTION

Make It Visual

Seeing our goals helps us believe they are reachable. Vision boards are a great way to organize and work toward things you want to accomplish. First, get a poster board or large piece of paper. Then, find images of the things you want in life. Maybe it's good grades, a healthy relationship, or to graduate from college. If you want it in your life, then it goes on the board. You can cut up magazines, sketch the images, or print them from a computer. Have fun with it and dream big. Once you have all the images, simply glue or tape them to the poster board or paper. Hang your masterpiece on your wall in a place where you will see it every day. Concentrate on the positive images each time you pass by.

What skills do you think are innate, not learned? Why do you think those skills can't be learned or taught?

_____

_____

_____

_____

_____

_____

_____

_____

_____

_____

_____

_____

_____

Actually, any skill can be learned, whether it's shooting a basketball or building a bookshelf. Think about a time where you told yourself that you were incapable of learning something. Why did you tell yourself that? Why didn't you believe you could learn the skill?

_____

_____

_____

_____

_____

_____

_____

_____

_____

_____

_____

_____

Creativity is a critical part of having a growth mindset. In the blank space below, draw a picture of anything you want. There is no right or wrong; just have fun and be creative!

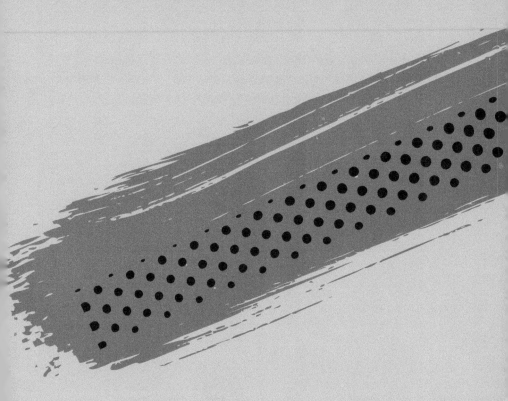

My absolute favorite kind of people in the world are people that are passionate about something.

—EMMA STONE

What does "being creative" mean to you? How do you see being creative as being connected to a growth mindset? Write down some ways you could express more creativity.

_____

_____

_____

_____

_____

_____

_____

_____

_____

_____

_____

_____

_____

Being aware of all things means we are not focused on any one thing. Explore a mindful thought process by describing your surroundings right now. Be super detailed and take your time. What did you notice?

_____

_____

_____

_____

_____

_____

_____

_____

_____

_____

_____

_____

_____

GROWTH MINDSET IN ACTION

Get Intentional

Being intentional means doing something on purpose, to get a specific outcome. Being intentional helps ensure we stay on track with our goals. Leading with intention daily helps us create and establish healthy habits. Healthy habits are the building blocks for future health, happiness, and fulfillment. For the next two weeks, try being intentional about your night-time routine. Commit to following the "three, two, one" plan: Three hours before bed, have your last meal or snack. Two hours before bed, put your work away. One hour before bed, stop all screen time (no texts! no scrolling!). Focus on letting your body relax and avoid stress so you can get a full night of restful sleep.

Healthy brains are built from healthy habits. What healthy habits do you have that help you feel your best? Maybe it's silencing your phone at bedtime, eating nutritious food, or getting time with friends. Are there new habits you could consider adopting?

_____

_____

_____

_____

_____

_____

_____

_____

_____

_____

_____

_____

Create two lists below: one listing your strengths (what you like about yourself) and the other listing your talents (what you are good at). Keep these lists in a place where you can see them, such as your desk, or take a picture of them with your phone. When you are doubting your abilities, look at these lists to remind your beautiful self what you are capable of.

Strengths

Talents

_____

_____

_____

_____

_____

_____

_____

_____

_____

_____

What core aspects of your personality do you see as being the most important tools to help you reach your future goals? Why?

_____

_____

_____

_____

_____

_____

_____

_____

_____

_____

_____

_____

_____

What I tell people is be the best version of yourself in anything that you do. You don't have to live anybody else's story.

—STEPH CURRY

If you could achieve anything in your life, what would it be? Why is this the most important thing to you? How does this goal align with your current values?

_____

_____

_____

_____

_____

_____

_____

_____

_____

_____

_____

_____

What are you most passionate about, and why? How can having a growth mindset allow you to live with more of your passions in your life?

_____

_____

_____

_____

_____

_____

_____

_____

_____

_____

_____

_____

Understanding our values is an important part of self-discovery, because our values help guide our behaviors. Take some time to create a list of your top ten values below. Some examples are adventurousness, creativity, fairness, generosity, honesty, kindness, persistence, working hard, etc.

1. _____

2. _____

3. _____

4. _____

5. _____

6. _____

7. _____

8. _____

9. _____

10. _____

GROWTH MINDSET IN ACTION

Mindful Moments

Mindfulness has been shown to reduce our stress and anxiety, give us a greater sense of purpose and clarity, and improve our memory and focus. Once you have the tools, it's not so difficult to build mindful moments into your day. Try this: Wherever you are right now, get into a comfortable position. Close your eyes if you like. Now, bring your focus to your breathing. Slowly inhale through your nose while counting to five. Then, slowly exhale out of your mouth while counting again to five. Repeat. Feel your chest rise and fall with each breath. Imagine tension releasing from your muscles with each exhalation. Do this for three to five minutes. Return to this exercise as often as you like. It can be super helpful before stressful events such as testing, trying new things, or having a difficult conversation.

Describe a time you didn't say or do something that you really wanted to in a social situation. What stopped you? Write down a good way for you to address that thinking, so you can be prepared to respond differently next time.

_____

_____

_____

_____

_____

_____

_____

_____

_____

_____

_____

_____

Who do you admire? It can be someone you know personally or a public figure. Write down what you value about them. How could you go about developing those qualities in yourself?

_____

_____

_____

_____

_____

_____

_____

_____

_____

_____

_____

_____

_____

A growth mindset is one of constant curiosity. Experiencing new things is an important part of feeding that curiosity. What does "being curious" mean to you? Describe the things you are curious about and how you might learn more about them.

_____

_____

_____

_____

_____

_____

_____

_____

_____

_____

_____

_____

PART TWO

YOUR PATHWAY TO CONFIDENCE

Let's work on building confidence! In this section, we'll explore how negative self-talk and limiting beliefs can derail your day-to-day interactions and long-term goals. You'll learn tools for replacing those negative habits with positivity and optimism. Those growth mindset tools—paired with practice, perseverance, and effort—can make you unstoppable.

Narratives are stories we tell ourselves about who we are and what we can accomplish. Sometimes self-limiting language creeps into our thoughts out of habit, without our fully realizing it. Those thoughts hold us back and keep us from reaching our goals. We may include phrases such as "I am not capable," "I can't do it," or "Nothing ever works out." Can you think of some self-limiting beliefs that you've made part of your story? When was the last time you thought them?

_____

_____

_____

_____

_____

_____

_____

_____

_____

_____

_____

_____

Look at those self-limiting beliefs you identified, and create positive self-talk statements that challenge them. For example, "I am not capable" could become "I am capable of doing anything."

_____

_____

_____

_____

_____

_____

_____

_____

_____

_____

_____

_____

_____

Positive self-talk is important in our everyday lives. If we make a habit out of thinking that we're not capable or aren't good enough, we start to believe it. Eventually, we convince ourselves those negative untruths are facts, and we lose the ability to reach our full potential. How do you think having ongoing negative thoughts affects your daily life, from getting dressed in the morning to trying to fall asleep at night? Does this represent a fixed or growth mindset, and why?

_____

_____

_____

_____

_____

_____

_____

_____

_____

_____

_____

_____

Your optimism will never be as powerful as it is in that exact moment when you want to give it up.

—AMANDA GORMAN

We often talk to ourselves more negatively than we would talk to our best friends. Let's stop being our own worst critics! What do you achieve when you talk negatively to yourself? What makes you believe that these thoughts are true?

_____

_____

_____

_____

_____

_____

_____

_____

_____

_____

_____

_____

_____

Imagine a friend saw that you were in need. Write yourself a note of encouragement as if it were from them. This is how you should be talking to yourself every day!

_____

_____

_____

_____

_____

_____

_____

_____

_____

_____

_____

_____

Worry steals your opportunities for joy and happiness, because it keeps you focused on the future and things outside of your control. To calm yourself the next time you're worried, think about only what you can change or affect. Explain why the second half of this thought turns it into a growth mindset: "Oh no, it might rain! But if it rains, we can move the party indoors."

_____

_____

_____

_____

_____

_____

_____

_____

_____

_____

_____

_____

_____

GROWTH MINDSET IN ACTION

The Amazing You!

You are an amazing person who has an incredible and unique set of skills and abilities. The question is not whether that statement is true but whether you believe it. Grab a piece of paper and a pen or pencil and write down five separate affirmations, or positive statements, about yourself. Maybe you'll write "I am intelligent" or "I am creative." It doesn't matter what the statements are, as long as they are positive. Once you have those five things written down, stand in front of a mirror and say them to yourself out loud while looking yourself in the eye. To really improve your confidence, do this daily and mix up the affirmations. It's time to start being honest about how amazing you are!

Write a letter to your younger self about a hard time they will face and what they will need to know to overcome it. Observe that you have already learned this lesson. How can you work on applying it in the future?

_____

_____

_____

_____

_____

_____

_____

_____

_____

_____

_____

_____

Write about an experience that made you feel proud and confident in yourself. What was it about that situation that allowed you to succeed? Have you incorporated that approach since? Why or why not?

_____

_____

_____

_____

_____

_____

_____

_____

_____

_____

_____

_____

Explain why these statements hurt your ability to create a growth mindset:

1. It's not like you are smart enough to figure it out.

2. There is no way you can pull this off.

3. You just don't have the talent.

_____

_____

_____

_____

_____

_____

_____

_____

_____

_____

_____

_____

We all have fallen into the trap of negative self-talk. Oftentimes it comes in the form of generalizations. The good news is that you can identify this tendency and change it. Choose three specific negative statements you've recently told yourself, and turn them into positive statements. Instead of "I am stupid," for example, change it to "I have a hard time with schoolwork, but I am really good at programming." The key is to focus on your strengths and avoid "all-or-nothing" thinking.

_____

_____

_____

_____

_____

_____

_____

_____

_____

_____

_____

GROWTH MINDSET IN ACTION
The Power of Positivity

Sometimes in life we need to get out of our thoughts and make an effort to give to others. For this exercise, I want you to make someone *else* feel wonderful about themselves. I want you to think of a close friend or family member. Next, I want you to think of everything you love and appreciate about them. Think of their strengths and abilities. Once you have your mind filled with all those positive thoughts about them, either call, email, snap, or text all these amazing thoughts you just had about them. Pay attention to how good it feels to encourage another person and brighten their day. You always have that power. Imagine how good it would feel to use it regularly!

What do you obsess about? Explore the ways in which obsessing causes anxiety and feeds negative thinking. Is it that all-or-nothing thinking again? Does obsessing help you achieve your goals?

_____

_____

_____

_____

_____

_____

_____

_____

_____

_____

_____

_____

_____

Write one goal you have been disappointed about not reaching, such as "I haven't learned to whistle." Now add the word "yet" at the end. Do you see how making it a "yet statement" brings you back to believing the goal is attainable?

_____

_____

_____

_____

_____

_____

_____

_____

_____

_____

_____

_____

Think about how you compare yourself to others—they could be people from your life or from social media. Write about what you think those comparisons do to your confidence.

_____

_____

_____

_____

_____

_____

_____

_____

_____

_____

_____

_____

_____

The advice that I wish
I would have given myself is
to not care about what other
people are thinking.

—CHARLIE PUTH

What kind of feeling does social media leave you with? Do you think it helps you build a growth mindset? Why or why not?

_____

_____

_____

_____

_____

_____

_____

_____

_____

_____

_____

_____

What does it mean to you to be courageous? Share an experience where you displayed bravery. What caused you to set aside your fears?

_____

_____

_____

_____

_____

_____

_____

_____

_____

_____

_____

_____

_____

Look over the list of positive self-statements below, and circle three that speak to you the loudest. Write about why you chose each one.

I am able to accomplish my goals because I control my effort.

I am a good friend and someone people can rely on.

I am a good person, and people are lucky to know me.

I am not defined by my mistakes.

I can learn new things and get better at the things I love.

I deserve good things because I work hard and always give my best.

I have a great sense of humor and am a joy to be around.

I have the power to be happy, no matter the circumstance.

I take on any new challenge that is presented to me.

Other people's beliefs don't mean I can't. I can do anything.

_____

_____

_____

_____

_____

_____

GROWTH MINDSET IN ACTION

Strength and Confidence

In order to develop a growth mindset, you must first learn to view yourself in a positive way. So often we look at ourselves through the lens of what we aren't good at or what we haven't done well. Start to change that filter by intentionally focusing on a positive aspect of yourself. Stand tall and close your eyes. Make sure you are standing with confidence and strength—don't slouch! Say the following statement to yourself, out loud, five times, with confidence and belief: "I am an amazing person who is capable of achieving my dreams, because I work hard and am willing to learn." It might take saying it a few times to memorize it. Write it out on a slip of paper and keep it handy for times when you need to remind yourself!

Share a story about a time you stepped out of your comfort zone. Maybe you tried a new food or wore different clothes. Was it a positive experience?

_____

_____

_____

_____

_____

_____

_____

_____

_____

_____

_____

_____

_____

Do you ever feel like you play it safe? What are the internal messages that make you avoid taking the risk of stepping outside your comfort zone?

_____

_____

_____

_____

_____

_____

_____

_____

_____

_____

_____

_____

_____

We often live in our comfort zones because we don't want to push ourselves to do things that make us uncomfortable. To challenge that, create a list of ten things you can do over the next month that will help you try new things and discover what you are capable of doing. Maybe it's talking to someone new at lunch, entering a talent contest, or finishing writing in this journal. Be creative and have fun!

1. _____

2. _____

3. _____

4. _____

5. _____

6. _____

7. _____

8. _____

9. _____

10. _____

I thought highly of myself growing up. I still do. There's not really much somebody can say to me to bring down my confidence or anything.

—A$AP ROCKY

Healthy risks are those risks that don't carry the potential to harm ourselves or others, either emotionally or physically. Sometimes taking risks can feel overwhelming because we don't know what the outcome will be. Write about a healthy risk you can take this week and why it's worth taking.

_____

_____

_____

_____

_____

_____

_____

_____

_____

_____

_____

_____

_____

What are examples of healthy risks and unhealthy risks? Why do you think healthy risks are part of a growth mindset?

_____

_____

_____

_____

_____

_____

_____

_____

_____

_____

_____

_____

_____

When you look back at your life when you are older, what do you want people to remember about you? Are you currently on track to live that life? What can you do to make sure you get or stay on that track?

_____

_____

_____

_____

_____

_____

_____

_____

_____

_____

_____

_____

_____

GROWTH MINDSET IN ACTION

Accept Yourself

How often we compare ourselves to others! "She's better looking than me," or "He's funnier than me," or "They're smarter than me." All comparisons do is fuel insecurities and make you think that you're not enough just as you are. You can stop that fixed way of thinking by not comparing yourself to others. Okay, maybe that feels like an impossible task, but there are ways to help limit the number of times you think negatively about yourself when you compare. When you notice your thoughts start to tell a story about why someone is better than you or more of something that you want to be, quickly shift your attention to one thing that you love about yourself and repeat it. Remind yourself that *you are enough*! You can go even deeper by reminding yourself that you are incredible just the way you are and that you are *more than* enough. Get creative with the messages you give yourself!

Have you ever thought something was impossible, only to reach that goal at a later point? What advice would you give to someone who doesn't believe it's possible to reach their goal? Did you give yourself that same advice?

_____

_____

_____

_____

_____

_____

_____

_____

_____

_____

_____

_____

_____

Imagine what it's like learning to read. You see all these differ-ent shapes in a row and they each have their own sound? Well, somehow *you* learned how to read—and you were probably only four or five years old! You never thought, "Oh, there's no way!" or "I can never do it." You just did it! What other amazing things have you learned since you were little? Write a note telling your younger self how proud you are of you!

_____

_____

_____

_____

_____

_____

_____

_____

_____

_____

Living authentically means finding things that make you happy, believing you can accomplish your goals, and putting it all into action to live your best life. Create a list of three small changes you could make to live your life in a more authentic way. Maybe you can research a hobby you want to try, start each day with an affirmation, or reduce the time you spend on social media. Pay attention to identifying changes that will help you focus on your strengths.

_____

_____

_____

_____

_____

_____

_____

_____

_____

_____

_____

_____

PART THREE

THE TRIUMPH OF TRYING AGAIN

So often in life we think that success is only about doing something perfectly the first time. In this section, you will learn that long-term growth comes from the lessons we learn from mistakes and failures. Embrace these growth opportunities and develop the resiliency you need to succeed!

Do you feel bad when things don't work out, or do you try to find the good in the experience? What does failure mean to you?

_____

_____

_____

_____

_____

_____

_____

_____

_____

_____

_____

_____

Write about a time when you made a mistake that turned into an important life lesson. Maybe an injury taught you the best way to do something, or a broken relationship taught you what to look for next time. Do you think you could have learned this lesson without the mistake? Are you thankful for the experience? Why or why not?

_____

_____

_____

_____

_____

_____

_____

_____

_____

_____

_____

_____

Do mistakes cause you to dwell on negative thinking? For example, "Forget it, I'm not good enough," or "That figures, nothing ever works out." Create a message you can say to yourself that will allow you to let go of the negative thoughts you have when you make mistakes.

_____

_____

_____

_____

_____

_____

_____

_____

_____

_____

_____

We're all human at the end of the day, making mistakes. But learn[ing] from them is the key.

—KENDRICK LAMAR

Share a time when you made a mistake that negatively affected someone else. What did you do to forgive yourself? How can you commit to being more forgiving of yourself for your mistakes in the future?

_____

_____

_____

_____

_____

_____

_____

_____

_____

_____

_____

_____

_____

There is beauty in the journey, not only the destination! Why do you think some people enjoy the process and effort, whereas others are focused more on results? Which is most important to you, and why?

_____

_____

_____

_____

_____

_____

_____

_____

_____

_____

_____

_____

_____

Share a story about a time when you were proud of yourself for the effort you gave, even if the results weren't what you wanted. Did you need to work through some adversity along the way? Has this impacted your experiences since?

_____

_____

_____

_____

_____

_____

_____

_____

_____

_____

_____

_____

_____

GROWTH MINDSET IN ACTION

Success Planning

Are you feeling a bit stuck? If so, you may still be operating from a fixed mindset. Back in the first section, I asked you to think of something you've always wanted to do. Feel free to pick something new if you like—a new hobby or activity. Just make sure it's something exciting yet achievable. Now create a five-step plan to follow through on doing your chosen activity. For example, before you learn to play guitar, you need a guitar! You'll need to research where to borrow, rent, or purchase one. Once you have a guitar, you'll need to find a teacher or online lessons. Then you'll need to establish a practice schedule. Taking small steps moves you in the right direction—a growth mindset direction! Remember the growth mindset principle of practicing to improve. Don't let negative thoughts stop you. Meet yourself wherever your skill level is, and focus on getting better over time.

Perfection is an impossible ideal, because there is no such thing as perfect. Not only that, but you are the one who defines "perfect"—and that definition can keep changing. How do you think you can work to accept that perfection is not possible?

_____

_____

_____

_____

_____

_____

_____

_____

_____

_____

_____

_____

_____

Perceived failures can be our greatest teachers. Below, create a list of the top five lessons you have learned through failure that you could share with someone.

1. _____

   _____

   _____

2. _____

   _____

   _____

3. _____

   _____

   _____

4. _____

   _____

   _____

5. _____

   _____

   _____

Having a growth mindset means looking at ways to overcome challenges instead of giving up. What does the term "solution-focused" mean to you? What could you do to incorporate more solution-focused thinking in your life?

A student tries out for the school play but forgets their mono-
logue halfway into their audition. Brainstorm ways in which
this student could turn this into a positive outcome. What
encouraging message would help this student?

_____

_____

_____

_____

_____

_____

_____

_____

_____

_____

_____

_____

_____

GROWTH MINDSET IN ACTION

My Hero

We project so much onto the people we admire, but did you know that everyone faces adversity in life? This includes those who seem to have the easiest path through life. Identify one of your heroes and research their life. Specifically, investigate what failures they encountered on their journey toward success. Then look at what they did to meet that adversity. Are you doing the same thing when you make a mistake or encounter a failure? Start incorporating this growth mindset technique, and you'll be more like your role model than you thought you could be.

When have you approached a situation by trying to avoid failure? Did this ensure that you would, in fact, fail? Why did you care more about avoiding failure than giving it your all?

_____

_____

_____

_____

_____

_____

_____

_____

_____

_____

_____

_____

_____

What does the word "resilience" mean to you? How have you developed resilience in the past? How could you help someone else develop resilience?

_____

_____

_____

_____

_____

_____

_____

_____

_____

_____

_____

_____

_____

Share a time when life really knocked you down. What did you do in response to the setback? Did you get up and continue to fight, or did you give up? Would you do the same thing if it happened again? Why or why not?

_____

_____

_____

_____

_____

_____

_____

_____

_____

_____

_____

_____

_____

If you're an honest person, you'll make mistakes, but it'll be okay. The most interesting things happen after making mistakes.

—KRISTEN STEWART

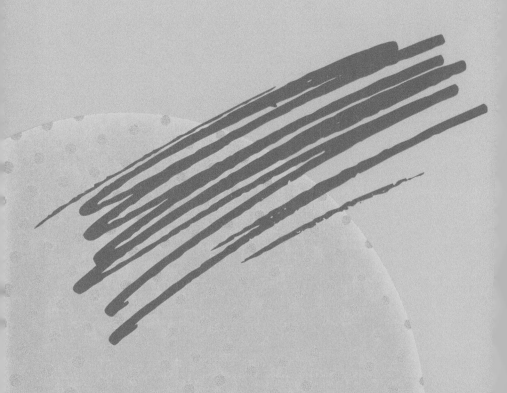

Practice makes perfect! Okay, maybe not perfect, but it defi-
nitely can improve your skills. Write about something you
practiced hard at and got better at. Were you surprised by the
improvement?

_____

_____

_____

_____

_____

_____

_____

_____

_____

_____

_____

_____

_____

If you are having challenges while practicing, what are you doing to build resiliency? As things get easier for you, what lessons are you learning about consistency?

_____

_____

_____

_____

_____

_____

_____

_____

_____

_____

_____

_____

_____

Share the most difficult feedback you've ever gotten. How did it make you feel? What did you do in response? How do you view that feedback now? Does it reinforce a growth mindset? Why or why not?

_____

_____

_____

_____

_____

_____

_____

_____

_____

_____

_____

_____

_____

GROWTH MINDSET IN ACTION

Turn Losses to Wins

How often do you try to actively avoid making mistakes or hide your failures because of what others might think? We are taught that failure and mistakes are bad. False! For this exercise, I want you to celebrate your failures. Well, not the failure itself, but what you gained from either making that mistake or taking a chance. Make a list of recent failures and lessons you've learned from them. Having a growth mindset means turning your losses into wins. You can do this by intentionally focusing on the growth. Don't be ashamed of your failures; embrace them for what they are—growth opportunities!

Have you ever received feedback that made you angry? Did you let that anger take control of your behavior? Or did you consider harnessing the anger to try harder and improve? Which choice is in alignment with a growth mindset, and why?

_____

_____

_____

_____

_____

_____

_____

_____

_____

_____

_____

_____

_____

How do you deal with the frustration of setbacks? Check the boxes next to the things you will do to apply a growth mindset to future setbacks. You can also write your own ideas in the blank spaces at the bottom.

- ☐ Be thankful for the experience
- ☐ Celebrate your effort
- ☐ Create a plan to do better next time
- ☐ Eliminate negative self-talk
- ☐ Give yourself affirmations
- ☐ Identify areas of needed growth
- ☐ Identify the positive lesson
- ☐ Know next time can be different
- ☐ Not compare yourself to others
- ☐ Practice self-care
- ☐ Seek feedback

_____

_____

_____

_____

_____

_____

Share a time when you felt rejected. What did you do in response? Was it a healthy way to cope? What would you do differently in the future?

_____

_____

_____

_____

_____

_____

_____

_____

_____

_____

_____

_____

_____

**Remember your
struggles along the way are
only meant to shape you for
your purpose.**

—*CHADWICK BOSEMAN*

If a friend came to you feeling bad about rejection, what would you tell them? Why do you think this would be an important message for them to hear?

_____

_____

_____

_____

_____

_____

_____

_____

_____

_____

_____

_____

_____

When faced with a competition, what thoughts and feelings do you have? Do you try to avoid the situation or try to prove you're the best?

_____

_____

_____

_____

_____

_____

_____

_____

_____

_____

_____

_____

What do you think is the healthiest way to deal with competition? Does it bring out the best in you, or does it make you want to win at all costs? Which option is part of a growth mindset? If you don't currently have a healthy perspective on competition, what could you do to adopt one?

_____

_____

_____

_____

_____

_____

_____

_____

_____

_____

_____

_____

GROWTH MINDSET IN ACTION

Dopamine Detox

Social media is a great way to keep in touch with others. But it can be a very overwhelming and toxic place. Whether it's encouraging negative comparisons or stealing your time that could be spent on more fulfilling endeavors, social media affects your daily life in detrimental ways. To break free of those impacts, try a social media detox. Commit to not checking your phone or going online for the next twelve hours. I know it will be hard to resist the temptation, but you got this! As you go through the detox, pay attention to anxious thoughts and how much social media affects the way you feel. Sometimes we don't even realize how much emotional control we give to external things. This is a simple way to begin to take your control back. It may be hard, but it's so worth it. Periodically build in these detox periods to reset your emotional life.

Everyone has emotional triggers—specific things that happen that make us feel a certain way. It's like when someone criticizes us in a harsh tone, and we feel sad or angry. Knowing what your triggers are can help you change the way you react and feel when they happen. Write down the five most frequent triggers you have for anxiety and stress, such as being called on in class, big assignments, group projects, sports, asking parents for help, social situations, etc. How might you prepare yourself to be less reactive next time?

1. _____

_____

2. _____

_____

3. _____

_____

4. _____

_____

5. _____

_____

Identify some of the best coping skills (such as meditation, deep breathing, or stopping comparisons) you can utilize to reduce your levels of stress and anxiety.

1. _____

_____

2. _____

_____

3. _____

_____

4. _____

_____

5. _____

_____

It is super important to be intentional about loving yourself, because it helps you develop resiliency in the face of adversity. You become stronger! Below, circle five ways in which you can incorporate self-love.

Creating art	Reading a book
Dancing	Reflecting on how you've improved
Daydreaming	
Exercising	Remembering the words of loving people
Going on a hike	Singing
Going on a picnic	Sitting outdoors
Laughing out loud	Taking a warm bath/shower
Listening to music	
Making a list of tasks/goals	Talking with a friend
Meditating	Thinking about pleasant events
Playing an instrument	Wearing nice clothes
Playing sports	

PART FOUR

A WORLD OF POSSIBILITIES

Get ready to believe that *anything* is possible. In this section, you'll engage your creative self to dream big and embrace endless possibilities. Using a growth mindset framework, you'll uncover your deepest passions and identify the steps to pursue them. You are more capable than you think!

When we dream about our future, we engage in a growth mindset by believing that all things are possible. What dreams do you have for your near future? Your adult future? Do you believe that you will realize them? Why or why not?

_____

_____

_____

_____

_____

_____

_____

_____

_____

_____

_____

_____

When we zero in on our goals, it's important to consider the steps we must take to get there. Goals can be short-term, like waking up earlier this week, or long-term, like training for a physical activity or learning a new skill. Write down at least three short-term goals and three long-term goals you have.

Short-Term Goals

1. _____

_____

2. _____

_____

3. _____

_____

Long-Term Goals

1. _____

_____

2. _____

_____

3. _____

_____

Select the long-term goal that you feel most passionate about, and write down what you can do daily, weekly, and monthly to help you reach it. If your goal is to get a job after graduating, for example, you could check the internet daily for ideas on what to do, research interesting companies weekly, and net-work with one new professional connection monthly.

Daily

_____

_____

_____

Weekly

_____

_____

_____

Monthly

_____

_____

_____

Maybe you're not meant to fit in. Maybe you're supposed to stand out.

—TAYLOR SWIFT

In the space below, write down five to ten things that inspire or interest you. Then list three ways you can incorporate them into your week.

_____

_____

_____

_____

_____

_____

_____

_____

_____

_____

_____

_____

Dreaming big is an important aspect of having a growth mindset. List one giant, crazy dream of yours (Play in the NBA! Be a platinum-selling rap artist! Fly to Mars!) and some ways you could actually make it happen.

_____

_____

_____

_____

_____

_____

_____

_____

_____

_____

_____

_____

Imagine that a friend had a major setback as they were working to achieve a goal. Write out how you might try to inspire them to keep going.

_____

_____

_____

_____

_____

_____

_____

_____

_____

_____

_____

_____

_____

GROWTH MINDSET IN ACTION

Growth Opportunities

Learning how to accept feedback is an important part of developing a growth mindset. Let's work on seeing criticism as an opportunity to learn and grow, and not feeling bad when you make a mistake. Reach out to a family member or a friend and ask them where they think you could improve. When they give you this feedback, *listen* without interrupting. Pay attention to your thoughts. Thank them for their feedback. Take a few minutes to stay in a place of gratitude for what they said and get excited that you were just given an opportunity to grow. Since you now have something you can improve, create a step-by-step plan to make some positive changes.

Creating a plan ensures that you stay on track to meet your goals. Write about a time when you benefited from having a plan. Do you think you would have reached the goal without the plan?

_____

_____

_____

_____

_____

_____

_____

_____

_____

_____

_____

_____

_____

Why is creating and executing plans important in developing a growth mindset? Do you think planning is an important part of reaching your goals? Or is it better to just "see what happens"? Why?

_____

_____

_____

_____

_____

_____

_____

_____

_____

_____

_____

_____

_____

What are your biggest distractions, and how do they get in the way of reaching your goals? What are some ways you could eliminate or minimize these distractions?

_____

_____

_____

_____

_____

_____

_____

_____

_____

_____

_____

_____

_____

Do you think you are self-disciplined? Could you get better? Circle strategies to prioritize tasks that need to get accomplished. Use the blank lines at the end to create your own.

Ask for help

Check in when feeling overwhelmed

Close all unrelated web pages

Create a list of tasks for each goal

Create an incentive for completing each task

Get a snack before you start

Put your phone in another room

Set daily goals

Text friends that you won't be available for the next hour

Turn a task into a game

Turn off the TV when working

_____

_____

_____

_____

_____

_____

GROWTH MINDSET IN ACTION

Taking Care

Staying in a growth mindset requires you to take good care of yourself. Sleep, exercise, and nutrition are all vital parts of functioning at your best. Which areas could you do a better job in? Remember, it's about progress and not perfection, so focus on small changes at first. Over time, those small changes will all add up to big changes and new habits. This week, choose one self-care goal/change. Next week, add one nutritional goal/change. The week after, add one physical activity goal/change. At the end of the month, you should see that those changes have given you the focus and energy to be your best.

With creative expression, the emphasis should be on the process, not the end product. List three creative outlets you admire, such as photography, journaling, crocheting, song-writing, etc. What do you think the creator learns during the creative process?

_____

_____

_____

_____

_____

_____

_____

_____

_____

_____

_____

_____

Rigidity, or refusing to change, is the hallmark of a fixed mind-set. Engaging in creative activities stops our tendency to be a perfectionist and allows us to explore different parts of ourselves. What are your current creative outlets? How often do you engage in them?

Write about a time when you were proud about something you created. What did you create? What did you learn about yourself during the process?

_____

_____

_____

_____

_____

_____

_____

_____

_____

_____

_____

_____

*Don't let the noise of others'
opinions drown out your own
inner voice.*

—STEVE JOBS

We've talked about the beauty of the journey, not the destination. What do you enjoy about the journey of your passions as you make your way to the destination? If you knit, for example, what is it about knitting that makes it as or more wonderful than the finished hat or scarf?

_____

_____

_____

_____

_____

_____

_____

_____

_____

_____

_____

From the list below, circle all the strengths, gifts, and characteristics that you possess and most value. Why do you value these aspects of yourself?

- Adventurous
- Ambitious
- Artistic
- Athletic
- Compassionate
- Creative
- Empathetic
- Giving
- Goal oriented
- Good communicator

- Good friend
- Helpful
- Honest
- Independent
- Intelligent
- Leader
- Motivated
- Passionate
- Sense of humor
- Thoughtful

_____

_____

_____

_____

_____

_____

How will you use the strengths you circled to create the life you want? How will these attributes help you in a career, a hobby, or some other situation?

_____

_____

_____

_____

_____

_____

_____

_____

_____

_____

_____

_____

_____

GROWTH MINDSET IN ACTION

Boundary Setting

Have you ever felt pressure to conform? Maybe it was going along with something a friend wanted you to do or feeling pressured by a social media trend. Well, this exercise is all about setting boundaries and knowing when to say no. Think about something going on in your life right now that makes you a little uncomfortable. Over this next week, focus on setting boundaries and saying no to those harmful situations. Give yourself permission to simply say no. It's okay to tell a friend you are busy or to simply delete that popular app for the next couple days. Practice good self-care by prioritizing what's in your best interests.

Write about a time when you needed to ask for help to accomplish a goal. Why did you need help? How did asking for help make you feel? Has it become easier for you to ask for help since? Why or why not?

_____

_____

_____

_____

_____

_____

_____

_____

_____

_____

_____

_____

_____

Having a growth mindset means knowing that we don't always have all the answers, and that is okay. We aren't supposed to know everything! Write about your greatest mentor, best coach, or another trusted adult and what you have learned from them.

_____

_____

_____

_____

_____

_____

_____

_____

_____

_____

_____

_____

Teamwork makes the dream work! Successful teamwork can require many skills: defining roles, delegating responsibilities, showing leadership, listening effectively, and brainstorming contributions. Write about a time that you were part of a group that worked well together. What were your strengths? What were the strengths of others in the group? How did those strengths together make for a better outcome than if only one of you had worked on the project?

_____

_____

_____

_____

_____

_____

_____

_____

_____

_____

_____

Don't ever doubt yourselves or waste a second of your life. It's too short, and you're too special.

—ARIANA GRANDE

When working on a team or in a group, what do you think are the best ways to motivate people to work hard? How would you try to motivate someone who wasn't putting in their full effort?

_____

_____

_____

_____

_____

_____

_____

_____

_____

_____

_____

_____

Exploring new opportunities pushes us to grow and challenge ourselves to develop new skills. Write about a time when you took advantage of a new opportunity. Maybe you tried out for a new sport or introduced yourself to a newcomer. How did the experience help you grow?

_____

_____

_____

_____

_____

_____

_____

_____

_____

_____

_____

_____

Write about a time when you were faced with a major change. What was your first response to the change? What did you learn from the experience?

_____

_____

_____

_____

_____

_____

_____

_____

_____

_____

_____

_____

_____

GROWTH MINDSET IN ACTION

Opposite to Emotion

This activity is for a time when you may be feeling angry or sad about something you experienced. It's called "acting opposite to emotion." It's not complicated, but it may feel hard to do, and that's okay. After all, growth is hard work, isn't it? Imagine a moment when you felt angry or sad. Maybe a friend was mean to you, or you couldn't do the thing you were hoping to do. Does the memory make you feel sad or angry? Now do the opposite: Think of something that made you laugh or feel good, like the last hug you had or joke you heard. If you aren't sure what the opposite emotion is, then just think of any positive feeling. Now that you are remembering the opposite emotion of anger or sadness, are you feeling better? It may feel weird or awkward at first, but it really will get easier each time you do it. This is a tool you can return to any time you want to release negative feelings.

Learning a growth mindset means making changes to thoughts and actions that used to keep you in a fixed mindset. What has change meant to you? Do you embrace it or fear it? How do your thoughts on change affect your mindset?

You've put a lot of time into considering your thinking process over the course of this journal. What aspects of your life do you think will be positively impacted by your exploration here?

_____

_____

_____

_____

_____

_____

_____

_____

_____

_____

_____

_____

_____

Look back through this journal and mark the prompts, quotes, and exercises that were most impactful. Write the page numbers below and the biggest takeaways from those pages. Now you can use this list as a quick reference for all the things you've learned and the ways you have strengthened your growth mindset! You've done a great job!

_____

_____

_____

_____

_____

_____

_____

_____

_____

_____

_____

_____

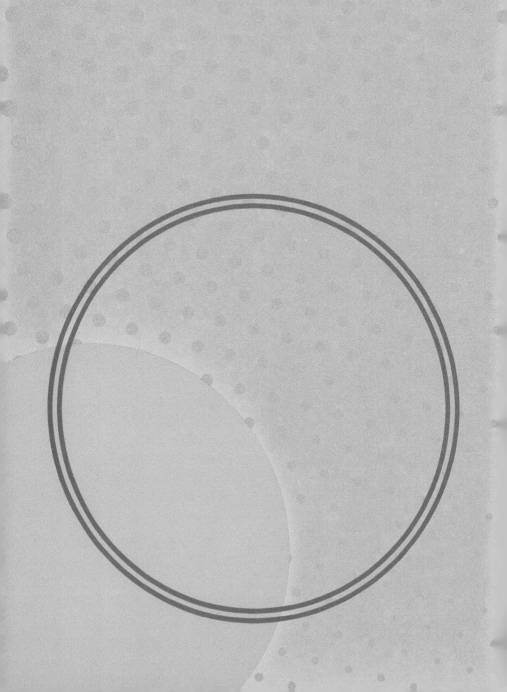

RESOURCES

Books

52-Week Feeling Journal for Teens: Daily Reflection, Expression, and 5-Minute Mindfulness Moments by Tiffany Ruelaz, PhD, LPC, CDBT

The 5-Minute Mindfulness Journal for Teens: Practices to Improve Focus, Relieve Anxiety, and Find Calm by Kristina Dingus Keuhlen, PhD, LMFT

Essential Stress Reduction Workbook for Teens: CBT and Mindfulness Tools to Soothe Stress and Cultivate Calm by Dr. Carla Cirilli Andrews, PsyD

Feeling Better: CBT Workbook for Teens: Essential Skills and Activities to Help You Manage Moods, Boost Self-Esteem, and Conquer Anxiety by Rachel Hutt, PhD

Inspirational Quotes for Teens: Daily Wisdom to Boost Motivation, Positivity, and Self-Confidence by Christopher Taylor, MA, LMFT

Self-Esteem Tools for Teens: A Modern Guide to Conquer Your Inner Critic and Realize Your True Self-Worth by Megan MacCutcheon, LPC

The Teens' Growth Mindset Workbook: Embrace Challenges, Build Resilience, and Achieve Your Goals by Ellen Weber, PhD

The Ultimate Self-Esteem Workbook for Teens: Overcome Insecurity, Defeat Your Inner Critic, and Live Confidently by Megan MacCutcheon, LPC

Online

Center for Humane Technology
The youth toolkit on this site offers insights on how social
media works.
Humanetech.com/youth

Clifton StrengthsExplorer
This site provides a comprehensive assessment tool for teens to
identify their strengths, as well as how to use these strengths to
help them succeed in school.
Strengths-explorer.com

"Grit: The Power of Passion and Perseverance"
TED Talk by Angela Lee Duckworth, April 2013
A discussion about the power of grit and a growth mindset in
helping kids maintain perseverance.
Ted.com/talks/angela_lee_duckworth_grit_the_power_of
_passion_and_perseverance

Headspace Guide to Meditation
Based on the popular meditation app Headspace, this series
provides guidance and the basics for developing a meditation
practice.
Netflix.com/title/81280926

InsightTimer
Free website and app for developing mindfulness habits to reduce stress and anxiety.
Insighttimer.com

Nemours TeensHealth
This site provides information on how to address common mental health struggles in teens and difficulties families face.
Kidshealth.org/en/teens/your-mind

"Challenging Negative Self-Talk," Youth Empowerment by Youth Era
This web page provides easy-to-use techniques to eliminate negative self-talk in teens.
Youthempowerment.com/challenging-negative-self-talk

Acknowledgments

A huge thank-you to my wife and kids for allowing me the space to work on this journal. And a special thanks to the team at Callisto Media for the opportunity to create something that I hope encourages a lot of young people to believe they are capable of achieving their dreams.

About the Author

 **Christopher Taylor, MA, LMFT,** is a therapist, author, and speaker with twenty years of experience working with teens. By believing that anything is possible, he found his purpose: to help heal and inspire young people to meet their own challenges head-on. Although he is grateful for his fulfilling work, his greatest joy is being a husband to his amazing wife and a father to his two incredible daughters.

Printed in the USA
CPSIA information can be obtained
at www.ICGtesting.com
LVHW021456160524
780487LV00007B/17

9 781685 392420